Reasons to Vote for Democrats

A Comprehensive Guide

MICHAEL J. KNOWLES

Threshold Editions

New York   London   Toronto   Sydney   New Delhi

Threshold Editions
An Imprint of Simon & Schuster, Inc.
1230 Avenue of the Americas
New York, NY 10020

Copyright © 2017 by Michael J. Knowles
Originally self-published in 2017

First Threshold Editions trade paperback edition April 2017

THRESHOLD EDITIONS and colophon are trademarks of Simon & Schuster, Inc.

For information about special discounts for bulk purchases, please contact Simon & Schuster Special Sales at 1-866-506-1949 or business@simonandschuster.com

The Simon & Schuster Speakers Bureau can bring authors to your live event. For more information or to book an event contact the Simon & Schuster Speakers Bureau at 1-866-248-3049 or visit our website at www.simonspeakers.com.

Manufactured in the United States of America

10 9 8 7 6 5 4 3 2 1

Library of Congress Cataloging-in-Publication Data is available.

ISBN 978-1-5011-8012-5

I have written my work, not as an essay which is to win the applause of the moment, but as a possession for all time.

—Thucydides

CONTENTS

Reasons to Vote for Democrats

CHAPTER 1

Economics

Reasons to Vote for Democrats

Economics

Reasons to Vote for Democrats

Reasons to Vote for Democrats

Economics

Economics

Economics

Reasons to Vote for Democrats

12

Economics

Reasons to Vote for Democrats

Economics

Economics

Reasons to Vote for Democrats

Economics

Economics

CHAPTER 2

Foreign Policy

Foreign Policy

Reasons to Vote for Democrats

Foreign Policy

Reasons to Vote for Democrats

Foreign Policy

Foreign Policy

Reasons to Vote for Democrats

Foreign Policy

Reasons to Vote for Democrats

Foreign Policy

Reasons to Vote for Democrats

Foreign Policy

Reasons to Vote for Democrats

Reasons to Vote for Democrats

Foreign Policy

Civil Rights

Civil Rights

Civil Rights

Civil Rights

Civil Rights

Civil Rights

Civil Rights

Reasons to Vote for Democrats

Civil Rights

Reasons to Vote for Democrats

Civil Rights

65

Reasons to Vote for Democrats

Civil Rights

Reasons to Vote for Democrats

Civil Rights

CHAPTER 4

Education

Education

Reasons to Vote for Democrats

Education

Education

Education

Education

Education

Reasons to Vote for Democrats

Education

Education

Education

Education

Education

CHAPTER 5

Homeland Security

Homeland Security

Reasons to Vote for Democrats

Reasons to Vote for Democrats

Homeland Security

Homeland Security

Homeland Security

CHAPTER 6

Energy

Energy

Reasons to Vote for Democrats

Energy

Energy

Energy

Reasons to Vote for Democrats

Energy

Energy

Energy

Reasons to Vote for Democrats

Energy

137

Energy

Reasons to Vote for Democrats

Energy

Energy

CHAPTER 7

Jobs

Jobs

Jobs

Jobs

Reasons to Vote for Democrats

Jobs

Jobs

157

Reasons to Vote for Democrats

Jobs

Reasons to Vote for Democrats

Jobs

Jobs

Jobs

Jobs

CHAPTER 8

Crime

Crime

Crime

Reasons to Vote for Democrats

Crime

Crime

Crime

Reasons to Vote for Democrats

Crime

Crime

Crime

Crime

Crime

Crime

CHAPTER 9

Immigration

Reasons to Vote for Democrats

Immigration

Immigration

Reasons to Vote for Democrats

Immigration

Immigration

Immigration

Immigration

205

Immigration

Immigration

Immigration

Immigration

Immigration

Values and Principles

Values and Principles

Values and Principles

Reasons to Vote for Democrats

Values and Principles

Values and Principles

Values and Principles

Values and Principles

Values and Principles

Reasons to Vote for Democrats

Values and Principles

Reasons to Vote for Democrats

Values and Principles

Values and Principles

BIBLIOGRAPHY

Alinsky, Saul. *Rules for Radicals: A Pragmatic Primer for Realistic Radicals*. New York: Vintage, 1971.

Berg, A. Scott. *Wilson*. New York: Berkley Books, 2014.

Bernstein, Carl. *A Woman in Charge: The Life of Hillary Rodham Clinton*. London: Vintage, 2008.

Black, Edwin. *War Against the Weak: Eugenics and America's Campaign to Create a Master Race*. New York: Dialog Press, 2012.

Blight, David. *Race and Reunion: The Civil War in American Memory*. Cambridge, MA: Belknap, 2002.

Bourne, Peter G. *Jimmy Carter: A Comprehensive Biography from Plains to Post-Presidency*. New York: Scribner, 1997.

Brackett, Elizabeth. *Pay to Play: How Rod Blagojevich Turned Political Corruption into a National Sideshow*. Lanham, MD: Ivan R. Dee, 2009.

Brands, H. W. *Reagan: The Life*. New York: Anchor, 2016.

Bullard, Sara. *The Ku Klux Klan: A History of Racism and Violence*. Darby: Diane Publishing Co., 1996.

Byrd, Robert C. *Robert C. Byrd: Child of the Appalachian Coalfields*. Morgantown: West Virginia University Press, 2005.

Caro, Robert. *Master of the Senate*. New York: Vintage, 2003.

———. *Means of Ascent*. New York: Vintage, 1991.

———. *The Passage of Power*. New York: Vintage, 2013.

———. *The Path to Power*. New York: Vintage, 1990.

Catton, Bruce. *A Stillness at Appomattox*. New York: Anchor, 1953.

———. *Mr. Lincoln's Army*. New York: Anchor, 1990.

———. *The Centennial History of the Civil War, 1861–65*. New York: Doubleday, 1961.

Chesterton, Gilbert Keith. *Eugenics and Other Evils*. London: Cassell and Company, 1922.

Clements, Kendrick A. *The Presidency of Woodrow Wilson*. Lawrence: University Press of Kansas, 1992.

Cooper, John Milton. *Woodrow Wilson: A Biography*. London: Vintage, 2011.

Creighton, Margaret. *The Colors of Courage: Gettysburg's Forgotten History—Immigrants, Women, and African Americans in the Civil War's Defining Battle*. New York: Basic Books, 2006.

Dallek, Robert. *Lyndon B. Johnson: Portrait of a President*. New York: Oxford University Press, 2004.

Damore, Leo. *Senatorial Privilege: The Chappaquiddick Cover-up*. Washington, D.C.: Regnery Publishing, 1988.

Fahs, Alice. *The Imagined Civil War: Popular Literature of the North & South, 1861–1865*. Chapel Hill: University of North Carolina Press, 2003.

Faust, Drew Gilpin. *This Republic of Suffering: Death and the American Civil War*. London: Vintage Press, 2009.

Fehrenbacher, Don. *The Dred Scott Case: Its Significance in American Law and Politics*. New York: Oxford University Press, 2001.

Fitzgerald, Michael. *Urban Emancipation: Popular Politics in Reconstruction Mobile, 1860–1890*. Baton Rouge: Louisiana State University Press, 2002.

Foner, Eric. *A Short History of Reconstruction*. New York: Harper Perennial, 2015.

Foote, Shelby. *The Civil War: A Narrative*. New York: Vintage Books, 1986.

Gettys, Embry Martin. *A History of the Democratic Party in Congress from 1897 to 1905*. Stanford, CA: Leland Stanford Junior University, 1932.

Grant, George. *Killer Angel: A Biography of Planned Parenthood's Margaret Sanger*. Nashville: Cumberland House Publishing, 2001.

Guelzo, Allen C. *Abraham Lincoln: Redeemer President*. Grand Rapids, MI: Eerdmans, 2002.

Hahn, Steven. *A Nation Under Our Feet: Black Political Struggles in the Rural South from Slavery to the Great Migration*. Cambridge, MA: Belknap, 2005.

Harris, William C. *With Charity for All: Lincoln and the Restoration of the Union*. Lexington: University Press of Kentucky, 1999.

Hazlitt, Henry. *Economics in One Lesson: The Shortest and Surest Way to Understand Basic Economics*. New York: Crown Publishing, 1959.

Holt, Michael. *The Rise and Fall of the American Whig Party: Jacksonian Politics and the Onset of the Civil War*. New York: Oxford University Press, 1999.

Leonard, Thomas C. *Illiberal Reformers: Race, Eugenics, and American Economics in the Progressive Era*. Princeton, NJ: Princeton University Press, 2017.

McGlone, Robert. *John Brown's War Against Slavery*. New York: Cambridge University Press, 2009.

McPherson, James. *For Cause and Comrades: Why Men Fought in the Civil War*. New York: Oxford University Press, 1998.

Moynihan, Daniel Patrick. *The Negro Family: A Case for National Action*. Washington, D.C.: U.S. Department of Labor, 1965.

Neubeck, Kenneth J. and Noel A. Cazenave. *Welfare Racism: Playing the Race Card Against America's Poor*. Abringdon-on-Thames, UK: Routledge, 2001.

Nelson, Donald Frederick. *Chappaquiddick Tragedy: Kennedy's Second Passenger Revealed*. Gretna, LA: Pelican, 2016.

Nevins, Allan. *Ordeal of the Union*. New York: Collier, 1992.

———. *The Emergence of Lincoln*. New York: Scribner's, 1950.

———. *The War for the Union*. New York: Scribner's, 1971.

Pestritto, Ronald J. *Woodrow Wilson and the Roots of Modern Liberalism*. Lanham, MD: Rowman & Littlefield, 2005.

Peterson, David J. *Revoking the Moral Order: The Ideology of Positivism and the Vienna Circle*. Lanham, MD: Lexington Books, 1999.

Potter, David M. *The Impending Crisis*. New York: Harper Perennial, 2011.

Price, Joann F. *Barack Obama: A Biography*. Santa Barbara, CA: Greenwood, 2008.

Rable, George C. *Fredericksburg! Fredericksburg!* Chapel Hill: University of North Carolina Press, 2012.

Richardson, Heather Cox. *To Make Men Free: A History of the Republican Party*. New York: Basic Books, 2014.

Roberts, Russell. *A History of the Democratic Party*. Hallandale, FL: Mitchell Lane Publishers, 2012.

Royko, Mike. *Boss: Richard J. Daley of Chicago*. New York: Plume, 1988.

Sanger, Margaret. *Woman and the New Race*. Elkhart, IN: Truth Publishing Company, 1921.

Schweizer, Peter. *Clinton Cash: The Untold Story of How and Why Foreign Governments and Businesses Helped Make Bill and Hillary Rich*. New York: Harper Collins, 2016.

Selfa, Lance. *The Democrats: A Critical History*. New York: Haymarket Books, 2012.

Sieracki, Bernard. *A Just Cause: The Impeachment and Removal of Governor Rod Blagojevich*. Carbondale: Southern Illinois University Press, 2015.

Stampp, Kenneth. *The Peculiar Institution*. London: Vintage Press, 1989.

Stout, Harry S. *Upon the Altar of the Nation: A Moral History of the Civil War*. London: Penguin Books, 2007.

Summers, Mark Wahlgren. *A Dangerous Stir: Fear, Paranoia, and the Making of Reconstruction*. Chapel Hill: University of North Carolina Press, 2014.

Tedrow, Richard L. and Thomas L. Tedrow. *Death at Chappaquiddick*. Gretna, LA: Pelican, 1980.

Wade, Wyn Craig. *The Fiery Cross: The Ku Klux Klan in America*. New York: Oxford University Press, 1998.

Walsh, Michael. *The People v. the Democratic Party*. New York: Encounter Books, 2012.

Wiley, Bell Irvin. *The Life of Billy Yank*. Baton Rouge: Louisiana State University Press, 2008.

———. *The Life of Johnny Reb*. Baton Rouge: Louisiana State University Press, 2008.

Wormser, Richard. *The Rise and Fall of Jim Crow*. New York: St. Martin's Press, 2003.